A Guide to Assist You And Your Parents in the Aging Process

By

Mona R. Meyers

Acknowledgement

When I began to talk about the "aging issues" along with various situations that always seem to come up relating to our aging mother, I start to jot down a few thoughts. My sisters, Joyce and Barbara, would also say to me, "boy Mona, I want you to take care of me and be in my corner", they cheered me on and encouraged me to write this guide. As our Mother's primary caregiver, I want to thank my sisters for always supporting me. So thank you, thank you! To our son Todd, my wonderful "daughter" Meaghan, our grand-children Jack and Keira, you light up our life with joy and happiness. To my dearest friends, Chris, Mary and Sandee thank you for always being there, I am so blessed that you are in my life.

A special thank you to Dr. Rolf Elhers, Dr. Robert Adamson, Dr. Brian Jaski and the outstanding nurses and staff at Sharp Memorial Hospital in San Diego, who over the past 15 years have provided my mother with unsurpassed care, skill and love.

To all my friends and family who have shared their personal experiences.

Lastly, to my wonderful husband Bob. You are truly an officer and a gentleman, my deepest gratitude for your unconditional love.

Dedicated

To my Mother
Dorothy Ann Holcomb

I am so proud to be your daughter. You have taught me so very much that I cannot even begin to put into words. Throughout your life you have shown courage, strength and determination which have been tested over and over with the countless life-threatening medical conditions. I have had the honor and privilege to be part of this journey and to be your friend, daughter, caregiver and now "parent".

Testimonials

Mona,

Thank you for our many conversations. Since we last spoke, I have a list all the medications that Mom is taking and information for all of her previous surgeries. This information came in handy when we paid a visit to her new physician. I had all this information itemized and this streamlined filling out "all" of her new paperwork. The office receptionist was very impressed! Once again, thank-you!!!

MaryAnn

Mona,

I can't begin to thank-you! I feel as if I am getting a handle on Mom's medicine and her health care issues. I have made a spread sheet, like you suggested and distributed this list to Ray and David so when Mom pays them each a visit they will have this information available to them if needed. I update the spread sheet each time Mom's medicine is changed. My brothers appreciate the heads up since they didn't know everything and the list is very helpful. Again, great idea and thanks.

Jane

Mona,

Thank-you, thank you! When Dad fell and broke his hip, we immediately had the information for the emergency room workers and staff. Under these trying circumstances, we were able to think clearly and provide all of his med's and insurance information.

Thank-you and I want to wish you the best of luck on the book. The information that you have provided is needed for us "baby boomers" who are becoming providers for our parents!

Steve

Table of Contents

CHAPTER 1

Why Am I Writing This Guide?

A Guide to Assist You and Your Parents in the Aging Process

My experiences have run the gambit of 1) having a father pass away with cancer at the early age of 54, 2) a father-in-law who died suddenly of a heart attack at the age of 42, 3) a mother-in-law with health issues who needed assisted living then nursing home care and 4) a mother who has had colon and lung cancer, aorta valve replacement along with heart bypass surgery to which I have been her primary caregiver for over 20 years (she has been in cancer remission for 10 years and is currently 87 years young).

My husband and I needed to travel to arrange for his mother to go into an assisted living facility. (You can only accomplish so much over the phone). My sister was going to stay with my mother. Due to the various medical situations and issues, I would make a list of doctors, dietary restrictions, administering of her medications, etc. The conversation then evolved into "I was not really aware that she had so many medical issues and that I needed to know so much detail." I then realized that even though we talk at great length and I keep her up to date on our mother's condition she really, really, really didn't know or understand the effort required in the day-to-day caregiving.

Then it struck me that I had accumulated a great deal of knowledge over the years in dealing with health and aging issues of our parents and this is why I am writing this Guide. I have numerous friends, family members and co-workers that have asked me about my experiences, who are facing similar issues and would like to gain insight into the world of assisting our aging parents. We have learned so very much and have experienced many life changing events. We have gone from what we thought was prepared, but in reality unprepared, to for now what is really prepared.

One of the key elements in dealing with these issues has been knowledge. I have learned by trial and error on what it is like to be the primary caregiver for not only an aging mother but one who has had a variety of medical issues over the years. Not only have I learned through this process but have been educated by listening to other family members and friends as they are facing similar issues with their parent(s). Everyone needs to share information on what they have learned along the path to assisting their parent(s). Friends have often called and ask "how do you do it?" or "what do I need to know to aid my parent(s)?" and "who do I call?" This knowledge has taken the form of learning about medical history of the parent(s), family medical history, financial issues, day to day living issues and dealing with sibling(s).

I would like to think this book is not only for the children of parent(s) but for our parent(s) also. The informational forms provided in the back of the book can be used as a guide to understanding not only medical history but financial and general information that is important to not only our parent(s) but even for ourselves.

The book's purpose is designed not only to assist the primary caregiver but to enable other sibling(s) and our parent(s) in forming a partnership with each other. This is the time for all the baggage between sibling(s) and parent(s) to be put aside. The focus is how to communicate and work with our parent's during this aging process. We as sibling(s) need to demonstrate to our parent's we can be trusted with their medical and financial information and we can show a willingness to put aside all past issues. If you have the discussion with your parent(s) and they are uncomfortable discussing the financial aspects with you, then request they see a lawyer to develop a financial plan or review their current plan.

When writing this book, it has taken various forms as to the type of information provided and not wanting to scare people off about the health care issues facing our parents but to give a roadmap of one person's journey in assisting my family, extended family and friends. Not all families will encounter the situations discussed in this book nor will they have brothers or sisters and maybe there are older individuals who have no children but a favorite niece or nephew.

I would like to think this book is not about having the "talk" or how to start the "talk" about issues before it's too late to address them but more of thinking along the lines of preparing for a natural disaster, such as tornado, hurricane, earthquake or fire. After having experienced earthquakes and mandatory evacuations, I'm here to tell you being prepared is so very important. In some cases, you will only have time to gather up your most important items. It is a good preparedness option to provide copies of these important documents to other family members.

I have broken down this book into a few sections on various topics along with series of questions that everyone should ask themselves then determine how it applies to your particular situation. At the end of each section are a few key take away points. Again, this is just one person's roadmap but I feel a majority of us need to address these possible situations and be prepared as possible now rather than later.

CHAPTER 2

Learning about Our Parents

Do You Know The Answers To these Questions?

- ➤ Who are your parent(s) primary doctors?
- ➤ What medicines, supplements and in what dosage are your parent(s) taking?
- ➤ Do you know the brand name, the generic name or the nickname of the medicine?
- ➤ Are you authorized on behalf of your parent(s) to speak to the Health Insurance Company?
- ➤ What is the name of your parent(s) health insurance company; do you have contact information?
- ➤ What are your parent(s) allergies? Do they wear a medical alert bracelet?

> ➢ Can you provide medical history – surgeries, medical conditions along with immediate family medical information?
> ➢ Do you know where your parent(s) important papers are?

If you answered "no" to any of these questions and many of you will answer "no", then it is time for the "Parent Talk". This is the talk to have sooner than later with your parents. In fact, it may be time for the talk between you and your spouse since the same things apply to your situation. Regardless of your parents' age and physical condition, you need to be realistic and get informed, not only for yourself but most importantly for them. It is so important that you and they have the necessary information and tools to help assist making good health and living decisions.

These are just a sample of the questions that are facing the baby boomer generation as we begin dealing with our aging parent(s). They have taken care of us all their lives and now it has been passed to us in some cases to become the "parent" or the caregiver. If you have siblings, sometimes the caregiving is shared but in most cases, one sibling steps up to assist the parent(s). AARP reported there are more than 40 million Americans who are in some way being cared for by their baby boomer children who range in age between 40 -60 years old. This is an alarming fact.

Our parents were part of the greatest generation and because of that, it is important to take a step back to understand where our parent(s) are coming from. Because many of them lived thru the depression, they have higher tendencies to save money, keep possessions and can be very guarded in providing financial or medical information. Our parent(s) also display a strong sense of pride and respect and they have worked extremely hard over their lifetime. Keep in mind many of them were not offered a 401K or other forms of savings for later years. Most of them have limited savings; receive social security and possibly a pension. Their homes are usually paid off and they have a strict monthly budget. That is why they may be very reluctant to talk about finances.

This can be a joyous time for the siblings and will enable the process of working together with your parent(s) so much more enjoyable. This will help to recapture family memories and assist in rebuilding bridges not only with parent(s) but with other siblings if there have been issues in the past.

There is no greater gift than having a conversation with your parent(s) because they will not always be with us. A friend recently said to me, she had the best afternoon and evening with her dad because it was just the two of them talking and going to dinner. She indicated that she was going to take more time out of her busy schedule and do more one on one with her dad because he will not always be there for her.

As children, this information may give you a better perspective on our parent(s) lives. Because in this busy world today we can forget what came before.

Take A Ways:

> Take time to learn the answers to the questions at the beginning of this chapter.

➤ Learn more about my family medical history just not my parents.
➤ Take time to talk to my parent(s) about their lives. Let them reflect on their history.
➤ Now is the time to spend quality time with the parents. (Put down the Blackberry, I-Pads and Cell Phones).
➤ Update family photos, the family tree and pass along old family recipes.

C H A P T E R   3

Parents

Questions for parent(s)

> ➢ Do you know the name of your spouse's primary doctor?
> ➢ Do you know the medicines, supplements and dosages that your spouse takes?
> ➢ Do you carry with you information about allergies? Do you wear a medical bracelet?
> ➢ Can you provide medical history of your spouse?
> ➢ Do you carry emergency phone numbers with you?
> ➢ Do you know where your important papers are located? Are they in a fireproof cabinet or file?
> ➢ Is your home "fall" proofed?

➢ Parent(s) when you travel do you give an itinerary of your trip to someone as a point of contact or in case of emergency to anyone whether you are taking a train, bus, flying or driving to a location?

If you answered "No" to any of these questions then you are not alone. I asked these same questions to several friends and they answered "No" also. So it's just not parent(s) who need to have the answer to these questions and many more as they grow older but the baby boomers need to know also.

It is wonderful that the majority of the greatest generation is still busy, active, healthy, traveling, driving, working in their gardens, playing bridge, volunteering and living in their own home today: plus in some cases helping to raise their grandchildren or at least being a part of their lives. However the key is being prepared for the unexpected.

For so much of your lives, you have been in charge and managed to have the type of life style you have worked so hard for over the years to enjoy. You have sacrificed so much over the years in raising your family and assisted your children during your lifetime. Now may be the time to share information with your children about yourself. As parent (s) you do not need to feel as if your children are ganging up on you and asking questions that you might not be ready to answer but that they are concerned about your health and welfare.

This is not about losing your independence and your children thinking you can't take care of yourself. It's more a matter of preparing for the situations that may occur. Your children want to believe that you are invincible and nothing is going to happen to you. Everyone needs to recognize and understand that the aging process can be extremely difficult.

It is important to remember that a lot of people are going thru similar situations or maybe they have been forced to deal with these issues out of necessity, i.e., a broken hip which now requires surgery and probable care in a rehabilitation center.

Here is an example:

A family member was out house hunting and slipped on a flight of steps and broke his hip and was unconscious for a few minutes. Fortunately for him, he was found by someone who knew where he lived and was able to get help. This family member was close to home and did not have his wallet with him for identification or a cell phone with him. The lesson learned was always carry identification and emergency numbers.

Here are some helpful hints:

If you have a cell phone you can program in names under "ICE" which stands for "in case of emergency" and you can program in or add in the telephone number you want called.

I know this might be hard for some parent(s) but it's not because you can't do things for yourselves its preparing for the future in an orderly manner. The world is transforming and maybe sometime in the future you might need assistance whether it's from a family member, friend or neighbor. So therefore, it is essential that you maintain some type of record of not only medical information but your personal information as well.

One of the questions above is about "fall" proofing your house. No home can totally be fall proof but there are things you can do such as:

> Installing hand rails in the bathroom shower or even on the bath tub
> Maybe it's time to install a bath tub with a side door
> Installing hand rails to the entrances to your home from either the outside or from the garage area
> Install night lights in hallways and bathrooms
> If you have trouble with your knees and the bath toilet is too low, either add an extension to elevate the toilet seat or place risers on the side of the toilet
> Take an inventory of your house, whether it's a loose stone on the porch or patio or tree roots that are showing or the rugs are loose. Ask someone to fix it for you now.
> If you have a basement and a handrail only on one side maybe it's time to add another handrail
> Do you have some type of "lifeline" alert item which you can wear around your neck or a bracelet?
> Using a wheelchair or walker for your safety when out at the malls, grocery store or hotel. Everyone is in a hurry, talking on their phones or texting. It would be so easy to get knocked down or to miss a curb. Don't let pride or embarrassment to stand in the way of your safety.

These are just a few ideas and I know there are so many things other things you can and could do to "fall" proof your homes. By "fall" proofing your home you are hoping to prevent accidents so you can hopefully stay in your home longer.

This is no way means you are unable to care for yourself, it only means you are taking steps to ensure your safety as much as possible. My aunt who is 77 years old and lives by herself and who is in fairly good health has a lifeline alert necklace and wears it. This is in case she might need help if she is in her yard working or falls in the house and is unable to reach a telephone.

I know it can be difficult to discuss some issues with your children. The reason may be as simple and varied as being very private individuals, to being ashamed to have to ask for assistance or unwillingness to pick one child over another. In addition having this conversation does not mean your independence and freedom is starting to slip away. It's more of being prepared to assist either your spouse or children during a medical emergency.

Another example: This occurs more than anyone can imagine and a friend recently told me this story:

Sara's mother fell and hit her head and also broke her hip. When they took her to the hospital and ran a blood test prior to surgery, it was discovered that Sara's mother was taking a blood thinner and they needed to postpone surgery due to the possible excessive bleeding caused by the medication. Sara said that she never felt so out of touch and was embarrassed trying to answer questions at the hospital registration, such as does your mother have any allergies? She didn't know. What medications was her mother taking? She didn't know. And on and on it went with the questions. I am sure you get the picture. Sara said that due to her lack of information it could have been detrimental to her mother's care. Well, like she said you never think that anything is going to happen to your parents and it never hits home until it happens to you.

This experience could happen to anyone and occur any-place, whether you are at home, traveling with or without your spouse or even to a younger person. This is not just something that affects older individuals but everyone, young or old.

Parents, it is important that when talking whether it's to your children or friends about your medicine there are several things to keep in mind. Medicine today is known by its brand name, generic name and of course the nickname. When visiting your doctor, it is a good idea to take all your medicine bottles along with any supplement bottles in a bag for the doctor to review and verify you are taking the correct medicines.

Another example: Miscommunication between a child and his parents about the medicines they were taking.

The son asked about the medicines and dosages because he was concerned his mother was over medicating. She then gave him the generic names on the prescription bottles. While the doctor gave him the brand name of the medicine prescribed and when talking to his mother she would use the nickname. So, the son who lives out of state asked a family friend to stop by the house and write down the names on the prescriptions bottles. He then called the pharmacy and got the correct information. Yes, his mother was taking the right medicine but everyone was calling it something else. Such as: blood thinner, Warfarin, whose nickname is Coumadin or for cholesterol, Atorvastatin, whose nickname is Lipitor.

Parent(s) one of the questions that comes to mind is "are you snowbirds"? Do you and your spouse have a second home or vacation place where you visit for more than 1 month during the year? If so, do your children know the name of the location and who to get in contact with if they are unable to reach you? This adds a whole new dimension when discussing medical issues particular if you use a doctor in that area. So you can see it is important to share information with your children. I know I would want my parent(s) to continue to be active and enjoy life to its fullest without constantly having to be worried about my parents. By sharing this information there is a peace of mind for everyone.

If you are a snowbird or have moved to a new location, it is important that you have copies of all of your medical records from your prior doctor. This includes eye doctors, mammogram, etc., along with the names and addresses of all doctors, hospital (you might have used) and testing labs.

I think it is important for parents to be able to share with their children issues they are facing. As parent(s) you receive so much mail like advertisements for life insurance, health insurance, car and home insurance and other types of advertisements mixed in with your normal mail.

Another example:

Just recently my sister received a statement of benefits rejecting payment to her doctor for services. She had selected a doctor which was within her network plan and the services should have been covered. Well guess what, the office staff had not only coded the services wrong but had forwarded the statement to the secondary company for payment. My sister looked at the statement and decided that maybe this doctor was not in her network. However upon further review of the statement she found that it was from her secondary carrier. She then started the process of calling first the doctor's office, push 2 for billing information which gave her another number to call and then reaching the billing service. They were able to undo the error and re-bill the primary carrier. Now my sister is only 65, I can only imagine what an older person would be going through to correct this matter.

One of the issues not addressed in this section has been putting our financial house in order. Again this may be a difficult and highly personal matter for you as parent(s). You do not want to feel like you are favoring one child over another or maybe you are not willing to discuss this matter with any of your children. This is your decision to make with your spouse. However, if unwilling to discuss with your children then at least discuss with an attorney information about your financial situation. I have included in the back of this book a form what covers an inventory of your assets and liabilities along with whose names are on those accounts. This is only a guideline and I'm sure there are other items depending upon your financial situation which would impact this form. However, I think it's a great starting point for a discussion between spouse(s) about their situation and even with your children when you are ready.

One thing related to discussing the financial situation I would suggest is that the parent(s) go to their local bank first to see if they have a trust department or financial advisor that can assist them. The reason for suggesting the bank first or if you have a trusted financial advisor, attorney or CPA to recommend to your parents is because sometimes, elder individuals trust the wrong people and can lose their savings. I know you have read about this type of elder abuse. Remind your parent(s) about being careful and not giving a blank "power of attorney" to just anyone. It may take your parent(s) several meetings or meeting with different advisors to feel comfortable with the right advisor when dealing with their financial planning.

My sister is a retired banker and she would use this guideline when dealing with her customers. She always said using this type of guideline was a great way to start a conversation with her customers and allowed them to start making decisions not only about their personal banking but their small business future and who would inherit the business. She recommended that this form or guideline be reviewed annually because you might have added, closed or changed accounts along with reviewing who the authorized signer on these accounts is.

Again, this is all about being prepared for the unexpected. I have two examples to share with you:

Example One:

When my grandmother passed away, she had an insurance policy which named my mother and her sister as beneficiaries. When we applied for the death benefits, we found out that my grandfather who had passed away 15 years prior was still listed on the policy as a beneficiary. Therefore, we had to apply for a new certified death certificate for my grandfather before the policy benefits would be paid out to my aunt and mother. No one had thought about reviewing any of my grandmother's paperwork after my grandfather passed away to remove him from the policy.

Example Two:

After my mother-in-law passed away, my husband was executor of her will and responsible for finalizing everything. Just after everything was closed, he found out that his mother had a safety deposit box. He had to have an attorney get a court order to open the box since the authorized signers on the box had been his mother and two aunts. Both of the aunts had passed away several years prior. The cost was several hundred dollars to go through the legal process to be able to receive the contents.

Another thing as parent(s) you can do for your children and grandchildren is to set with a tape recorder or video camera and just discuss your lives and the lives of those around you. When working on a recent family tree and anecdotes about family members it became apparent that since my grandparents and their brothers and sisters had passed away that now so much of the family history is missing. This is a great opportunity to share with your family about your younger lives.

One thing we did with my grandmother, who lived to be 96, was to sit with her and go through her old china cabinet. It was full of little items which looked like junk to me but had special meanings to her. So we worked on the cabinet for days, marking the bottom of each item along with a brief history for each one. She was sharp as a tack and would remember clearly who gave her each item. It was a great gift to spend time with her and learn a little more family history. Not only did I learn more about her and her life but it was also a way to find out who she wanted to have what when she passed away. This way no questions were asked about her wishes. Not that we would have had a problem but it's another way to head off problems if you think there may be one within your family.

Take A Ways:

- ➢ Parents do not want to lose their independence or acknowledge that they may need assistance.
- ➢ Know the names of medicines being taken by spouse along with generic name and nickname.
- ➢ What can I do to fall proof my home?
- ➢ Don't be afraid to show information you received if you don't understand. It happens to everyone young and old alike.
- ➢ Am I prepared in case of an emergency?
- ➢ Are my important documents in one place? Are they in a fireproof safe or file of some type?
- ➢ Does my family have copies of important documents?
- ➢ This is your chance to set up different strategies and options.

CHAPTER 4

Sibling(s) Role

Do you know the answers to these questions and how they affect you?

- ➤ Do you know the medicines, supplements and dosages your parent(s) are taking?
- ➤ In the case of a medical emergency, who makes the decision regarding your parent(s) treatment?
- ➤ What is the name of your parent(s) primary doctor?
- ➤ Who is their health insurance carrier? Primary, secondary?
- ➤ What are the social security numbers of your parent(s)
- ➤ What are your parent(s) wishes?

> ➢ Do they want to be placed on life support?
> ➢ Have they purchased cemetery lots? If so, where and who do you contact.
> ➢ What do they want for a funeral?
> ➢ Are you aware of any unusual spending habits – impulsive purchases (i.e., TV Infomercials, Internet or Mail order buying)?

Again, if you answered "no" to any of these questions you are not alone. In today's ever changing families, there are more than sibling(s) involved in the care of an aging parent(s) because of deaths and divorces there are more and more blended families. There are the biological sibling(s) from an original marriage, biological sibling(s) from a new marriage, step-sibling(s) from other marriage, live-in partners and the list goes on depending on the family history. It is not a perfect world for families or sibling(s) I know we don't live in Mayberry, USA. Estrangements and disagreements happen in every family and between sibling(s) but this is the time to set aside these issues for the better good of supporting our aging parent(s).

This is why the dynamics for the sibling(s) and their points of view on how to work with each other and their parent(s) will come into play. This can be a very fragile area when beginning this process. These dynamics will be reflected not only in the immediate family circle but as part of each family's history and cultural backgrounds. This diversification may become evident when the sibling(s) arrange that first meeting between themselves. This can range from a family having daughters and sons only to a mixture of daughters and sons with varying ages, birth order, marital status, financial condition and where they live in proximity to the aging parent(s). Now try and add in the in-laws to this mix.

Some in-laws will not want to be involved because they are dealing with their own parent(s) or want no part of the process. That's all right. But it will be important that the in-laws be informed because what you as sibling(s) decide will in some cases may have a direct impact on them and their family. In some cases, because of the current economy issues or marital issues of a sibling they have had to move back in with the parents.

Over the years, I have observed these situations described above with family, friends and business associates. Every family has a story about their sibling(s), whether they are a close knit family or one is the group leader and takes charge of everything or it's a mixture of sibling(s) or in-laws working together to support the aging parent(s).

I know in my immediate family, one of the situations we faced is the differences in ages (seven years between each of us), marital status and location plus our place in the birth order. But the key to our success is we love each other, have always been close and only want the best for each other and our mother.

Every family has a birth order, i.e., oldest, middle and last. You know how that goes, "mom" or "dad" always liked you best; you got everything. I had hand me downs and I got nothing while the baby of the family got everything. If you know what I mean it occurs in every family. As the middle child in our family, my favorite phase was "I was deprived." This was not the case but it was a great line to use on my parents. In fact, my dad was the middle child in his family and I know he never felt deprived. This is the time to put all that baggage behind you at the front door when starting to meet because nothing good will come out of digging up the past. Its past history and everyone has made mistakes, misspoken, hurt some ones feelings, had too much to drink, reacted to some slight and has been that know it all. The focus must be on the current situation we are facing along with our parent(s).

As siblings this is our opportunity to spend time together and remember the good things in our family history. Remember too your children (the grandchildren) are watching how you handle the situation with grandmother and granddad, since one day you will be in your parent(s) place and relying on your children for assistance. The old adage, "what goes around comes around" needs to be remembered. This is the time for each sibling to set the example not only for each other but within their own family. To quote the tagline from Nike, **"Just Do It!"**

But how do we do it and how do we approach our parent(s). Remember your parent(s) may be reluctant to discuss their personal medical matters or even financial matters with their children. Some of the reasons may be as simply as explained in the parent chapter but worth repeating here. The parent(s) are very private individuals, to being ashamed to have to ask for assistance or unwillingness to pick one sibling over another. So the conversation with the parents must be held in calm and a non-threatening manner, this way the parent(s) will not feel like they are being ganged up on by their children. Maybe the next step after the siblings have communicated is one sibling approaches the parent(s) to open a dialogue with them about a meeting to discuss family issues.

How do we meet as sibling(s) and how do we start the meeting between ourselves. Here is a sample of talking points for the meeting between the sibling(s). This way there is an agenda and a more businesslike approach to the situation at hand and can hopefully assist in the conversation. This is just a sample of questions to be used between the sibling(s) and these talking points need to be adjusted for each family's situation and how you want to approach the matter.

Talking Points for the Meeting between the Sibling(s)

It is best to have a meeting with your sibling(s) before there are serious medical issues or financial issues with your parent(s).

- ➢ Establish ground rules on what needs to be accomplished and what the goals are between sibling(s).
- ➢ I would recommend that the first sibling(s) meeting needs to be sibling(s) only. No in-laws.
- ➢ The meeting with the parent(s) should be sibling(s) only or the sibling opening up the conversation with the parent(s). No in-laws.
- ➢ All issues and baggage between sibling(s) **must** be left at the door.
- ➢ No alcohol should be served. Remember, one word leads to another and before you know it World War III has broken out.
- ➢ The key issue is to have a calm discussion on how to approach your parent(s) and why you are having this conversation with them at this time. Use some of the examples in this guide or use your own examples.
- ➢ Treat the meeting between sibling(s) as a business meeting. Be open and frank about the situation.
- ➢ One of the keys is listening to what everyone is saying. Have an open mind and respect the various

points of views on how to handle the situation.
- ➤ If one sibling is currently the primary caregiver, then everyone needs to listen to what he or she has to say.
- ➤ If there are financial issues on why one sibling can't help out, then be upfront on whatever the issue maybe. Maybe they can assist in other ways.
- ➤ If sibling(s) live out of the area, then arrange a conference call or use meeting-on-line or Skype as a method of everyone being able to communicate during the process.
- ➤ One person should be taking some type of notes. Nothing fancy, but a statement of what was discussed, who will be handling various task gathering information and then communicating the results to everyone. This ensures that all the sibling(s) are involved and everyone is on the same page.
- ➤ A very important point is that the sibling(s) present a united front if everyone is meeting with the parent(s).

Note: I have not included the in-laws at the initial meeting between sibling(s) or with parent(s). The reason behind this is it adds more people to the mix and some in-laws do not want to be involved because they are dealing with their own parents or some are just not interested in addressing the parent(s) situation.

That's alright because maybe some of the sibling(s) don't want to be involved in this process either.

No matter what happens the in-laws and uninvolved sibling(s) will be affected either with their time, emotions or financially because everyone needs to work together to make this process as seamless as possible not only for themselves and their families but the parent(s).

The sibling assigned to the task of opening up a dialogue needs to explain the reasoning behind this request. It is to ensure that their wishes are understood by the family and what they want to happen in case of any emergency or natural disaster. This way the parent(s) will feel empowered and in control of what their wishes and needs are at this time in their lives. Maybe your parent(s) have not thought about these situations and will need time to digest the conversation.

Here is a sample of questions that might assist in jump starting the conversation with the parent(s):

- In a medical emergency, who will make the decisions?
- Who are your parent(s) doctors?
- Who is their insurance carrier? Primary, secondary?
- Who is authorized to talk to the insurance carriers on their behalf? Have the carriers been notified of that person's name?
- Is your medical history written down somewhere?
- Where are your important papers?
- Who has the medical power of attorney?
- What are your parent(s) wishes?
- Do they want to be placed on life support? Is there a DNR order in place?
- Have they purchased cemetery lots? If so, where and who do we contact?
- What do they want for a funeral?
- How do they want their obituary to be published?
- Is it to be a military funeral?
- Do they have a will or trust?
- Who is their attorney of record?

These are just a few questions to put to your parent(s) in the beginning phase of the conversation. There are so many other questions to be asked and you do not want to overload your parent(s) at one time with nothing but questions. The discussion needs to be more conversational and you need to let the conversation evolve. You never want to make your parent(s) feel "stupid" or "incompetent". However, the world is changing and sometimes it is hard for them to understand or catch on as quickly as they did when they were younger.

This way using some of the talking points or checklists included in the back of this book can serve as a guide for the conversion. In most cases, there is time for the discussion to occur over several months. What you are attempting to accomplish is getting your parent(s) thinking about issues and starting the planning process.

However, I believe the **most important issue is the medical information.** Someone other than the parent(s) need to have this information at their disposal and updating the medical information factsheet as needed. I know when we travel with my mother, not only do I carry the information but my sisters also have a copy of the medical information factsheet in case the unexpected happens. Again, it's being prepared that will make everyone's life much easier in an emergency.

You do not want to scare your parents into believing something is wrong or that they are unable to care for themselves. I prefer to think of this conversation more as having a peace of mind for myself that if the unexpected does occur I'm prepared along with my sibling(s) to act responsibly on behalf of my parents.

I mentioned in the questions above about cemetery lots, funeral insurance and what their wishes are if and when that time happens. I think this is a squeamish subject that no one wants to face. But it is a fact of life for everyone young and old. Recently when talking to a friend who had to have this conversation with her parents indicated, in fact they wanted their obituary to be more than just statistics put together at the last moment. They wanted to share their passions and favorite things in the obituary. The mother had been clipping out obituaries from the paper that she liked and was using them to fashion out her obituary. The parents had also planned out their funeral from the bible verses, songs and flowers. My friend was so shocked because they had already started planning but not sharing with their daughter because they didn't want her to be upset that something might be wrong with them. So you see your parents may be doing the same thing because they have been attending funerals of their friends and classmates.

Here is an example of siblings working together:

This is a family of six siblings, four daughters and two sons with parents who are still living in their own residence. However the mother has been very ill recently and has fallen and now needs a walker to get around. The siblings met and decided on a course of action after the initial hospital and rehabilitation center stay. The siblings are now having daily phone calls and rotating weekend visits to help around the house, running errands, grocery shopping, cleaning closets, and putting photo albums together along with taking mom out to the store or just spending time talking to mom. It's hard on the dad to do everything because he is not as steady on his feet and is a little afraid of falling himself. Plus it takes time getting the mother in and out of the car. The time the siblings are with the mother, it gives the dad a break and he can do a few things he would like to do or maybe visit with friends for a few hours. This way the burden, and it's not a burden, is spread out among the siblings to lend a hand. This works because the six siblings all live close by.

Take A Ways:

➤ How do I start to talk to my parent(s) and sibling(s) about understanding the medical facts of our parent(s) health but also the financial and day-to-day living issues facing the parent(s)?

➤ Everyone must work together and listen to everyone's point of view.

➤ Concentrate on what is important which is helping to understand the medical facts of our parents.

➤ Treat the meeting with sibling(s) as a business meeting and the reasoning behind the need for such a meeting.

➤ Do not gang up on the parent(s) but treat them with the respect and dignity they deserve.

➤ Reassure your parent(s) that the meeting is for all to be more informed and have important info available if needed.

CHAPTER 5

Primary Caregiver

According to Webster's Dictionary, "caregiver" means one who takes care of a child, invalid, etc. However, I want to expand that definition to mean being responsible for someone other than a child, invalid and include an aging parent(s). Caregivers can either be a family member, friend or a paid professional individual who lives with the aging parent(s) or the aging parents live with the family member caregiver and their family.

There are draw backs to being the primary caregiver because as my mother aged she started to have various medical issues. This takes a toll on everyone's life who is involved in her care. From various hospital stays, to after-care recovery, to a year of chemotherapy, medical tests, follow-up appointments and the list goes on and on. These tasks take on a different meaning because I was working full-time. So it involved scheduling around my work schedule and arranging to have time off when she was in the hospital. I would try to schedule appointments early in the morning for my mother so I would not have to take a lot of time off work. Even though my sister's would fly in to assist with mother; it was more the day-to-day issues that affected me and my family. It can definitely be a challenge when you are working outside the home, running a household, raising a family and being involved with various activities. Talk about trying to be the "Super Mom" to everyone!

The caregiver role is truly one of the toughest jobs, but can also be the most rewarding. As a caregiver, you may be taking care of your child and parents at the same time. You may be so focused on juggling many roles and responsibilities that you can be prone to what's called "Caregiving Stress Syndrome" which is the lack of adequate self-care.

As a primary caregiver we tend to put ourselves last on the "to do list". Everyone else and other things become the top priority. However, in order to reduce this stress, we must take care of ourselves also. We need to have some type of balance along with time for oneself and spouse in order to have a daily routine. The job of a family caregiver can be a 24/7 job depending on the condition of the aging parent and their needs. **So taking time for oneself is so very important**. This can be in the form of talking a quick walk, stretching or mediating are a few examples that are extremely important and valuable to your own wellness and peace of mind. Again, depending on the situation maybe, your doctor can recommend medical or in home services to assist the aging parent. Is there a senior citizens center in your town or a bus from the church that has senior activities? It is just as important for the aging parent(s) to get out of the house (if possible) as it is for the caregiver. If you don't have sibling(s) close by to assist maybe there is a teenager or family friend who would for a better choice of words "babysit" your parent(s) for a couple of hours so you and your spouse could have a few hours out.

At some point, you just want to be alone and you need some down time but since my mother is always with me it is difficult to tell her I need some time and space for a couple of hours. This is when you need to ask your sibling(s) for support. Maybe they can take the parent(s) out to dinner or to a grandchild's activity or maybe just spend the weekend at the house with the parent(s). I know my mother would be alright alone for an hour or so by herself or maybe I'm too protective of her and want to watch over her all the time; since we have become attached at the hip to each other.

As a primary caregiver I have learned from my own experience that giving her too much information whether it's about travel plans or doctor appointments or family events as she has gotten older, it's harder for her to remember things. So I have given my mother a calendar which we have marked up to include everyone's birthday and anniversaries along with three months of doctor, hair and nail appointments and projected travel plans. This way she feels like she is involved in what's happening to her and in her life. One of the tricks, I have learned instead of making multiple trips to the card store, she purchases all of her cards, three months in advance of the event and will address and stamp the envelopes. This way she will place a post-it on the envelope to know when to mail them. It will make your life just a little easier.

You know the "caregiver stress syndrome" does not just apply to the children who are taking care of aging parent(s) but also the spouse. It is very helpful to have a support system in place in order to relieve the caregiver for some personal time. Remember you are not alone in dealing with these situations. In searching the web, I came across several sites which may be useful to you: ARCH Respite Network, www.achrespite.org (a service that finds services and programs), Family Caregiver Alliance, www.caregiver.org (this is a state by state list of services) and there are many more websites to visit, so just type in "caregiver" and as you can see you are not alone and there is assistance available in your town.

Every caregiver does need an outlet for themselves and their family. It's important to remember to take care of yourself. This is not being selfish but is about your well-being and maintaining a healthy relationship with your supportive spouse and children. It's ok to say, "It's me time".

Here is an example of caregiver stress syndrome:

This is the condensed version of what happened to one family friend's parents. The father had developed Alzheimer disease and the wife became the full time caregiver. In the beginning it was alright but as time passed it became more and more difficult for the wife. She had looked into placing the husband in a facility but because they had saved little money over the years it was not an option. (See Chapter 7 for a better understanding of this type of situation). The wife took care of the husband for almost six years with help from their children and grandchildren but it took a toll and finally the husband was placed in an assisted living facility. He passed away several months later then within 9 months the wife passed away from exhaustion with a medical issue that if found earlier could have been cured and saved her life. The lesson learned is its ok to take care of you. You don't have to always be the strong person and the take charge individual because you are just as important to your family as the aging parent(s) is to you.

I am fortunate to be able to travel with my family. So I like to use the phrase, "no child left behind" when discussing a family trip because mother is always included in our plans. However there have been times when mother has stayed home and one of my sister's would fly over and stay with mother for a long weekend or even a week. Again my mantra is it's alright to do things by yourself or with your family without including the aging parent(s).

I have found that some airlines are better than others in assisting individuals that might require wheelchairs, walkers or have other issues when travelling by air. When you purchase tickets, you can indicate that you have special needs, such as requiring a wheelchair and it will be available at check-in or at your arrival gate. Also when purchasing airline tickets with assigned seats, think about where you want to sit, like upfront, closer to the restrooms, or in an area that has more leg room.

Even if the requirement for a wheelchair is not necessary, at times, it is a good idea to make use of a wheelchair for the safety of the parent (s) to avoid being knocked down and injured. This would be especially useful in crowded areas such as the mall, grocery, department stores and amusement parks.

In addition, when making hotel reservations you should to indicate to the staff any special requirements you might have. Also inquire if they have wheelchairs on site so you don't have to bring your own.

Take A Ways:

➤ As a primary caregiver it's alright to take time for yourself and for your family.

➤ Ask for assistance or support from sibling(s) or other friends and family.

➤ Don't be too hard on yourself when working with your parent(s) to solve problems.

➤ Try and keep the parent(s) active. Let them have an outlet also.

➤ Include the parent(s) in family outings. Don't make them feel like a burden.

➤ Know what works for you and your family when dealing with an aging parent(s) whether they live with you or in their own home.

➤ Read up on "caregiving stress syndrome" and feel good about yourself.

➤ Be pro-active in their care and search the web for organizations that can assist you or give you direction.

CHAPTER 6

Non-Caregiving Sibling(s)

Do you know the answers to these questions and how they affect you?

- ➤ Do I know were my parent(s) important papers are located?
- ➤ Do I know the names of my parent(s) doctors?
- ➤ Do I know what medicine, dosage and supplements my parent(s) are taking?
- ➤ If your parent(s) are able to travel have you invited your parent(s) to visit?
- ➤ If you live close by have you included your parent(s) in the lives of their grandchildren?
- ➤ Have you provided support to the primary sibling

caregiver?

➤ If your parent(s) still live by themselves do you stop by and visit?

➤ If your parent(s) still live in their home have you taken the time over the weekend to assist them in cleaning up the yard, gutters, closets, garage or getting their car washed?

➤ If your parent(s) still live by themselves is the house "fall proof?"

➤ Do you know of an outside handyman to do small repairs around your parent(s) home?

➤ Do you know the names of your parent(s) neighbors to reach in case of an emergency?

➤ Do you know the names of your parent(s) neighbors if they are snowbirds to reach in case of an emergency?

Again, if you answered "no" to any of these questions, then it's time for the talk between the primary caregiver and the other sibling(s) about how to share some of the duties, whether the parent(s) live with the caregiver or still by themselves.

If you are a non-caregiving sibling you are in the toughest of positions. Depending on if you live nearby or need to travel to visit parent(s), it is challenging for many reasons. First of all, do you feel left out of the process, knowing how to communicate with the caregiver and try to coordinate schedules if possible to take over that role for a long weekend or whenever possible. Do not revert to a child and allow your childhood baggage to creep into the current situation. Such as Mom and Dad always loved you more, maybe that was just in your own mind or even if they did this is your opportunity to really allow them to see the person that you have become. Estrangements and long lasting disagreements happen in every family and between siblings but again this is the time to set aside these issues for the better good of dealing with the issues facing our parent(s). As siblings this is an opportunity to spend time together and remember the good things in your family history.

Be supportive of the caregiving sibling and do not stand on the sidelines criticizing or second guessing the decisions which have been made. Keep in mind that your input and suggestions are always welcome but do not judge the situation.

One of my favorite examples is about the out of town sibling who only talks to the parent(s) a few minutes every couple of weeks and then will call the primary caregiver and say that the mom or dad sounded fine over the telephone and then flies in for a few days at the holidays. Everyone is on their best behavior and the parent(s) will act like everything is alright. The sibling leaves town and doesn't understand what the issues are with the parent(s) because everyone was laughing and having a good time and the parent(s) didn't mention anything. That's when the primary caregiver should tell the out of town sibling(s) let's trade places for a few days or a week and then you will witness what I'm talking about. It's making sure the parent(s) are at their scheduled doctor appointments or taking their medicine, correcting medical bills, paying their bills, taking them to the post office or driving them to the store to look around along with getting either their walker or wheelchair in and out of the car.

My younger sister calls herself the non-caregiving sibling. As we were writing this section on sibling(s) and the interaction between them she indicated that so many thoughts began racing through her mind about if she had to take care of our mother and reflecting on feeling inadequate as a sibling and a possible caregiver. As we discussed that is not the case with her. My sister adds love, humor and laughter to any situation and is always willing to drop everything to come to the aid of our mother.

How a family deals with the non-caregiving sibling may be much different in some families than that in other families. Each family needs to address the issue as it pertains to them and their situation.

The key is communication and support for the primary caregiver. It is not an easy task since in many cases the primary caregiver may have to stop working in order to assist the parent(s). Remember the old saying, "Don't judge me until you have walked a mile in my shoes" Non-caregiving sibling(s) can offer so much support by being there for the primary caregiver, offering their time and being that cheerleader for your sibling.

Take A Ways:

- ➢ Understanding your role as a non-sibling caregiver.
- ➢ Being involved in the process with the primary caregiver. This is one of the main reasons for the meeting with the sibling(s).
- ➢ Be supportive of the primary caregiver.
- ➢ Taking time out of your busy schedule to assist with your parent(s).

CHAPTER 7

Medical Information

Do you know the answers to these questions?

➢ What type of medical insurance coverage do your parent(s) currently have?
➢ What is the difference between Medicare and Medicaid?
➢ What is the difference between a senior residential home and an assisted living facility?
➢ What is the difference between home health care and a skilled nursing facility?
➢ What services and prescriptions are covered under your parent(s) medical plans?
➢ Do you know the cost of a professional in-home caregiver?

Again, many of you will answer "no" to these questions. That's alright because learning the answers will be as varied as the situation(s) currently facing your parent(s) and every situation will be different. The key is preparation and learning as much as possible and what is available under your parent(s) plan and what might be available in your area. In some cases, it might be beneficial to visit your parent(s) insurance agent or the local social security office to discuss the coverage's currently in the plan.

This is not an easy task for the family when dealing with aging parents. However, it is a fact of life that all children must face. This is a whole new realm to navigate for everyone involved. As our parent(s) age, they do not want to feel like a burden but they need assistance when dealing with doctors and insurance companies. Have you tried to read and understand the "Statement of Benefits" form from your own insurance company? Now imagine what your parents are facing since they may have both a primary insurance company, such as Social Security Medicare (Part A and B) or the original Medicare plan or may have optioned for the Part C which is the private insurance company coverage and a secondary insurance company or may have coverage from their prior employer under their pension plan. The drugs are covered under Part D. I suggest that you read about Medicare and its current coverage's. (www.Medicare.gov)

Confused yet? Now see how your parent(s) must feel. Whether you are a primary caregiver or non-caregiving sibling do you know about the different types of Medicare programs or insurance companies?

A key factor in discussing the medical situation and options is knowledge is power. The more information you have gathered the better to assist in the decision making process. Learn more now before you are faced with that emergency and will need the information. The examples discussed here are not to scare you and your parent(s) but to give you an idea of what I, members of my family and friends have experienced over the years. Every situation is different based upon medical conditions, location, financial situation and the time of the issue. I can't stress enough that everyone needs to prepare and take precautions in advance just as if a natural disaster had happened. You need to determine what is available now or if there are waiting lists at these facilities in your area for your parent(s) before the situation arises. You may not want to share this information with your parent(s) at this time but sharing among the siblings and in-laws will give greater pause when discussing and removing any misconceived ideas about what might be available. This is an every changing area of knowledge but again learning everything that is available will be of assistance.

One of the hardest issues is the understanding of "terminology" when not only talking to our parent(s), siblings and friends but in trying to figure out what everyone is talking about. Since so many of the terms we use are interchangeable but mean different things and coverage for our parent(s). As I have said before, everyone's situation is different and I by no means am an expert in this area. I can only share with you what my experiences have been and those of other family and friends.

I implore everyone, whether you are the caregiver or a sibling, to start this process of exploring what is available to your parent(s). Do not wait until it's too late and the need is immediate. Start searching the web and just type in "health care facilities" or check out the telephone directory in your local town for these types of facilities. Go and visit them, request information from them and pass the information along to your siblings or even to your parent(s) when you get to that point in the discussion.

Some examples are when discussing in-home care, housebound, skilled nursing homes, senior assisted living or independent living centers with supportive medical services with your siblings. Plus what is the difference between Medicare and Medicaid? Do you know the differences and what might be covered under Medicare? I do not have a lot of knowledge about this area except for a few experiences with my husband's late mother and a few family members and friends. I am by no means a professional in this area, but here are a few of the glossary explanation of terms from the Medicare program (as of July 2012) from their website:

> **Home Health Care** – Health care services and supplies a doctor decides you may receive in your home under a plan of care established by your doctor. Medicare only covers home health care on a limited basis as ordered by your doctor.
> **Skilled Nursing Facility (SNF)** – A nursing facility with the staff and equipment to give skilled nursing care and, in most cases, skilled rehabilitative services and other related health services.
> **Homebound** – To be homebound means: 1) leaving your home isn't recommended because of your condition, 2) Your condition keeps you from leaving home with help (like using a wheelchair or walker, needing special transportation or getting help from another person) and 3) Leaving home takes a considerable and taxing effort. You may leave home for medical treatment or short, infrequent absences for non-medical reasons, like attending religious services. You can still get home health care if you

attend adult day care.

➢ **Medicaid** – A joint Federal and state program that helps with medical costs for some people with limited income and resources. Medicaid programs vary from state to state, but most health care costs are covered if you qualify for both Medicare and Medicaid.

➢ **Medicare** – The Federal insurance health program for people who are age 65 and older, certain younger people with disabilities and people with End-Stage Renal Disease (permanent kidney failure requiring dialysis or transplant, sometimes called ESRD).

According to, Wikipedia, the free encyclopedia, assisted living residences and assisted living facilities (ALF) are defined as follows:

➢ **Assisted living residences and/or facilities** – Serve as an eldercare alternative for people for whom independent living is no longer appropriate but who do not need 24-hour medical care provided by a nursing home. This is for individuals who may need help with dressing, bathing, eating and toileting but not the 24 hour care.

Assisted living facilities fall somewhere between an independent living community and a skilled nursing facility in terms of the level of care provided.

Here is the real eye opener on the cost of assisted living facilities and it will depend on the types of services required by your parent(s), the price can range between $25,000 a year to more than $50,000 a year. This may be the base figure but you will need to add in for the extra services that may be needed by your parent(s) and add to this amount.

If we compare assisted living facilities with those called senior independent living centers. The "senior independent living centers" are residential apartments that allow for independent living with three meals a days, activities and a variety of amenities. These types of facilities can range in cost for a one resident studio for approximately $1,235.00 to a two bedroom apartment for $1,890.00 or if two residences the cost for a studio can range from $1,635.00 to a two bedroom for $2,290.00. The cost will vary from location to location and state by state. Several family members had lived in these types of facilities over the years, when one of the spouses passed away and was unable to continue living at home by themselves. Another family member used this type of facility while recovering from surgery and a stay in a rehab center, he wanted to see if he wanted to move out of his home and try this type of living arrangement. After a few months, he decided to move back home and "fall" proof his home.

Again, when selecting a new place, ask questions, explore all the costs associated with the facilities, such as the extra services, to have bathing and dressing assistance, personal laundry services, medication reminders and escort to meals and talk to people currently living there along with your parent(s) family doctor to determine if this is the type of facility he would recommend. Visit the websites of various senior independent living centers in your area to see what they charge. Again, take the time to visit these facilities for yourself and find out if this one of these might be the type of facility that your parent(s) would like.

It should be noted that the cost of assisted living is normally covered by the patient and/or their family. There are some health and long-term care insurance policies available that may cover some of the costs. Having said that, currently, the Medicare program **does not** cover the costs of assisted living facilities or the care they provide. Medicaid may cover continued stays in a nursing home. (Need to check because it will vary from state to state and only at approved facilities). However, Medicaid requires that the patient be "spent down" to a low asset level first; this means the parent(s) have to use all their life savings and sell their residence before being on Medicaid. You and your parent(s) need to see an attorney to discuss this issue and what the rules and regulations are for your particular state because they vary from state to state. Sometimes, you will hear the term "seven year" rule used which means that your parent(s) have had very low levels of income for the past seven years and no longer have any assets. Whether this is a myth or not when dealing with Medicaid, you need to check it out now before it's too late to take action.

In addition, if your parent(s) are going to move into some type of assisted living facility, please check it out first and ask questions.

Here is an example:

> My mother-in-law informed us she was ready to move into an assisted living facility. So my husband started asking questions about the facility, cost, doctors, activities but she assured us this was the one she wanted. Her response was many of her friends were living there and were very happy. So she felt comfortable even though the facility was about 20 minutes away from where she currently lived she was determined it was the right place. The

initial move in cost was several thousand dollars upfront but we felt if she was comfortable then we would pay the initial move in fees. Well, guess what, her primary doctor was not associated with this facility and she had to take transportation by van/ bus (which charged her $35 to $50 round trip) to visit her doctor once a month. Needless to say, she did not stay in that facility for any length of time. My husband ended up moving his mother to the right support facility for her that her doctors were associated with along with the ease of receiving dialysis.

The next example is complicated and has occurred over the past three years to a family friend. When describing what had occurred, I have taken the liberty of condensing down the events in concern for the confidentially of the family friend. After reading this characterization of the facts, you will have questions about why they are not doing something else. I can tell you the three siblings are smart and knowledgeable along with the fact they have investigated all avenues to assist with their mother's medical condition and her financial situation. It may be as simple as the mother's home is "under water" on the mortgage or other financial conditions. So in a nut shell, here is their story.

Example:

About three years ago the mother had a major stoke and was paralyzed on the left side. After she was able to come home, the first agency they dealt with charged them $40.00 an hour for 6 hours a day and only 5 days a week

($40.00 x 6 = $240.00 x 5 days = $1,200 a week x 4 weeks = $4,800 a month). The family took care of the mother the other hours of the day along with rotating the weekends. The family split the cost between themselves for the care.

As my friend reminded me, this did not cover medicines, wheelchair, hospital bed with air mattress that runs all the time to keep her from getting bed sores, etc. Medicare does cover some of these initial items. They have a house call doctor who will visit every three months so the medicines can be renewed along with an in-home tech that draws blood every three months for $40.00 a visit.

This was too much for the family to handle. They found a qualified person who would charge $140.00 a day and live in with the mother. The cost for the professional home caregiver is approximately $4,200 a month for 24/7care. Again, the family is splitting the bill. The family found out about a VA program for World War II widows and after months of dealing with that agency, they got approved for a $900.00 a month VA benefit payment. In addition, they found that through SSA/adult services that the live-in caregiver can go to several hours of classes, fill out a time sheet and send it in an gets paid. They were approved for 164 hours versus the 720 hours in a month for care at $9.52 an hour. The caregiver nets approximately $579.00 after taxes and union dues (required) bi-weekly and the family pays the difference to get the caregiver up to the daily rate.

As you can see from this example in home care is very expensive and I have only touched on the base care provided.

Here are two more examples:

A family friend fell and broke their leg which required surgery and a stay in a rehabilitation center for more than 90 days with around the clock care. As the daughter's told us, the cost was over $20,000 a month. When the mother returned home, she still required 24/7 care and had 3 professional caregivers rotating the 24/7 schedule at approximately $10,000 a month which works out to about $14.00 an hour. The daughters are splitting this cost and have been for the past year.

A business associate has a widowed father, who has trouble getting up and out of bed. So every morning a professional caregiver comes to the house and stays 4 hours to assist the dad with getting out of bed, bathing and fixing breakfast. The weekly cost of this is approximately $400.00 and the son is paying for it out of pocket.

I know these may seem like extreme cases, but I am sure if you start talking to friends and family you will found out that many families are dealing with this issue. We have not even tried to address the facts if the parent(s) have more serious medical illness.

These examples again are meant to provide awareness of issues that may be happening now or may occur in the future. So talk to your friends who have aging parent(s) who may have them in a facility or getting in home services and see if they will share their story with you. This is how you learn about the medical system and the problems facing all of us either now or in the future.

To find out additional information, check out the websites for these topics:

- www.medicare.gov
- American Geriatric Society
- Assisted Living Residences
- Eldercare (www.eldercare.gov)
- Homecare
- Independent living residences
- Medicaid by individual state
- Nursing homes
- Retirement villages

Take A Ways:

- Knowledge is power.
- Learn all you can about the medical programs available in your area.
- Visit an independent living residences and nursing homes in your area.
- Don't be afraid to ask questions when talking to family and friends.

CHAPTER 8

In Closing I Would Like To Offer Some Final Thoughts

➤ It is important to spend quality time with your parent(s).

➤ Do not make your parent(s) feel like they are a burden on you or anyone else.

➤ Do help them realize and reinforce the fact that they are a valued part of the family.

➤ Do not be afraid to travel with your parent(s) – be sure they have adequate medications for the trip (I recommend taking extra supplies in the case of unscheduled delays).

➤ Do not hesitate to ask doctors, pharmacists, medical technicians or insurance companies pertinent questions.

➤ Take ownership of the situation(s) and, if necessary, be persistent until you have the answers to your questions.

➤ Set a good example for your children and family.

➤ Doing what is right is not always easy.

➤ Be kind, be flexible, be informed and be compassionate.

➤ If you do all you can now you will not have any regrets later. No would of-could of-should of.

➤ Take it one day at a time.

➤ It is a privilege and honor to care for your parent(s).

CHAPTER 9

Forms and Information Checklists

General Medical History Information Sheet

For:_____

As of:_____

Social Security Number: _____
Date of Birth: _____

Medical Insurance Carrier: _____
Policy Number: _____
  Group Number: _____
  Secondary Insurance Carrier: _____
  Policy Number: _____
  Group Number: _____

(Take a copy of the medical cards for your records)
(Get business cards from all doctors)

Name of Primary Doctor: _____
Address: _____
Telephone Number: _____
Fax Number: _____

Name of all secondary doctors/addresses/telephone numbers:
Urologist
Cardiologist
Oncologist
Ophthalmologist
Geneticist
Dentist

List of all medicines, supplements, dosage and how many times taken a day:_____

_____

_____

_____

_____

List any medicines they are allergic to:_____

_____

_____

Prior Surgeries and dates:_____

_____

_____

_____

Questions:

Do they wear dentures/eye glasses/have pacemaker /artificial limbs, etc.?

Is there a medical power of attorney on file with the hospital?

Is there a DNR order on file with the hospital?

What is the family history for various diseases'? Like cancer, heart problems, etc. and on who's side of the family?

NOTE:

This is only a general information sheet and is not all inclusive of questions asked but it is a starting point in case of an emergency. I recommend that you get a copy of the most recent form completed at the doctor's office for more detailed information. I recommend you make copies of all insurance cards and get business cards of all doctors the parent(s) use. Also, I would pass this information sheet along to other sibling(s) and be sure your parent(s) has a copy for their records, in case you are not immediately available.

GENERAL TALKING POINTS

TO START CONVERSATION WITH PARENT(S)

Note this is not a complete list but are suggestions for talking points with your parent(s). Again, each situation is different.

- ➤ As your children do we have medical information about you in case of an emergency?
- ➤ Who are your doctors?
- ➤ What type of medicines, supplements and dosages are you taking?
- ➤ In a medical emergency, who will make the medical decisions for your care?
- ➤ What are your medical wishes?
- ➤ Do you want to be placed on life support or do you have a DNR order on file?
- ➤ Where are all your important papers? Like birth certificates, insurance policies, passports, wills, social security cards, divorce papers and any other important papers. Are they in a fireproof file?
- ➤ Who has extra keys to the house and cars?
- ➤ If you have an alarm system, what are the codes and password?
- ➤ As your children, do we know the names and telephone numbers of your neighbor's or closest friends in case of any emergency?
- ➤ Have you purchased cemetery lots? If so, what is the name, address, telephone number of the cemetery, your plot number or account number? Are the lots completely paid for?
- ➤ Do you have prepaid funeral insurance in place with the funeral home? If so, what is the name, address, telephone number and your policy number? It this policy completely paid?
- ➤ As your children, do we know what type of funeral

you want, flowers, song, how your obituary should read, is it a military funeral, if a military funeral who should receive the flag, etc.?

➤ Do you have any attorney? If so, who is it and what is their address and telephone number?

➤ If your parent(s) are snowbirds, do you have information on who to contact and address in case of an emergency?

➤ Ask your parent(s) if they have information about each other in regard to doctors and medicine questions.

General Information Worksheet (Page 1 of 4)

Name	Web Address	Log-In	Password	Account No.	Auto Debit
Alarm Company					
Home					
Life					
Airline Rewards/ Tickets					
American	www.aa.com				
Delta	www.delta.com				
Southwest	www.southwest.com				
United	www.united.com				
US Airways	www.usairways.com				
Bank/ investment Accounts					
Bank #1					
Bank #2					
Investment Accounts					

General Information Worksheet (Page 2 of 4)

	Web Address	Log-In	Password	Account No.	Auto Debit
Bills Paid On-Line					
Cable					
Credit Cards					
American Express					
MasterCard					
VISA					
Department Stores					
HOA -Primary Home					
HOA- Secondary Home					
Insurance					
Life					
Property					
Vehicle/ Vehicles					
Mortgage					
1st - primary home					
2nd - primary home					

General Information Worksheet (Page 3 of 4)

	Web Address	Log-In	Password	Account No.	Auto Debit
Newspapers					
Local					
USA Today					
WSJ					
Taxes					
Primary home					
Secondary home					
Timeshare					
Utilities					
Electric					
Trash					
Water/ Sewer					
Vacation Club					
Computer log-ins					
Mother					
Father					

General Information Worksheet (Page 4 of 4)

	Web Address	Log-In	Password	Account No.	Auto Debit
Misc Computer log-Ins					
Aol.com					
Facebook.com					
Toys 'R Us					
Telephones/ Cell Company					
ATT & T					
Sprint					
T-Mobile					
Verizon					

General Discussion for Survivor Checklist

This checklist is not an all-inclusive list but provides a starting point for what the survivors need to do and what matters need to be handled and possibly by whom.

- ➤ What funeral home is handling the funeral? If a military funeral, the funeral home director can be of assistance in arranging military honors.
- ➤ What are the names, addresses, telephone numbers and policy numbers for the life insurance companies?
- ➤ Who are the beneficiaries of these policies?
- ➤ Obtain a minimum of 5 to 6 certificated copies of the death certificates. It is always better to have more copies than might be necessary since copies will be needed to show proof of death for insurance policies and other retirement benefit programs. Normally provided for at a cost from the funeral home.
- ➤ What are the names, addresses, telephone numbers and policy numbers for the companies that provide auto and health insurance for the deceased?
- ➤ Survivors need to find out from the life insurance companies who are the beneficiary designations and request revision as appropriate.
- ➤ Contact the local Social Security office. Know the social security number of the deceased and the office will be able to provide you information on what actions need to be taken.
- ➤ If the deceased was a Veteran, contact the nearest Department of Veteran Affairs (VA) office. They will assist with applications for survivor benefits and entitlements. The VA or local American Legion or Veteran of Foreign Wars (VFW) posts will assist with a number of burial benefits for deceased military members. Know what branch of service, grade or rank and time of service in military of your parent(s).

65

If your parent(s) are retired military you need to always keep their **DD-214s**. This form is extremely important for veterans.

➤ What is the name of the deceased present or former employer(s) regarding possible insurance benefits (group coverage), life insurance, pension funds and any other entitlements?

➤ Notify creditors of death and check for possible insurance protection (mortgage insurance, etc.).

➤ Contact Department of Motor Vehicles for information on updating the registration and titling of all motor vehicles.

➤ Notify organizations the deceased belongs to (auto clubs, service organizations and publications) to remove name from mailing list and report death as applicable.

➤ Notify banks, credit unions, investment funds, etc., where the deceased had an account or joint account.

➤ If a widow or widower of a retired veteran, will need to update military identification at nearest military facility to reflect your new status.

➤ Update your Will, Power of Attorney, Durable Power of Attorney, and/or Living Will as necessary.

Family Income As of _____		
List Income and Expenses	**Husband**	<u>Wife</u>
Home of Household (present)		
Earned Income		
Social Security		
Pensions		
Investment Income		
Expenses of Household (present)		
List all monthly expenses, mortgages,		
taxes, ultiilties, HOA, insurance, etc.		
Expenses of Household (project for 5 years)		
Anticipated Extraordinary Future Income		
(stock options, inheritance, retirement benefits, etc.)		
Anticipated Extraordinary Future Expenses		
(health, education, home improvements, business		
Buy-out, etc.)		
Totals		

Family Information		
As of _____		
	Husband	**Wife**
Legal name as it should appear		
In documents		
Nickname (if any)		
Primary Residence Address		
Home Telephone Number		
Cell Telephone Number		
E-mail Address		
Business Name/ Address		
Business Telephone Number		
Date of Birth		
Place of Birth		

Forms and Information Checklists

	Husband	Wife
Date of Marriage		
Place of Marriage		
Prior Marriages Terminated		
By Death or Divorce – with Date		
Social Security Number		
Citizenship		

Assets Checklist (Page 1 of 6)

Assets as of		Owned by	Owned by	Owned	How Titled?
(Attach copy of Statements)	Amounts	Husband	Wife	Jointly	
ASSETS					
Residence Description					
Estimated Fair Market Value					
Outstanding Principal Balance					
Outstanding Equity Line Balance					
Real Estate - 2nd Home or Investment					
Estimated Fair Market Value					
Outstanding Principal Balance					
Outstanding Equity Line Balance					
Bank Accounts:					
Name of Bank/ Account Numbers					

Assets Checklist (Page 2 of 6)

	Amounts	Owned by Husband	Owned by Wife	Owned Jointly	How Titled?
Checking					
Savings					
Money Market					
Certificate of Deposit					
Life Insurance - Face Value					
Name of Company					
Policy Numbers					
Securities - Publicly traded Stocks/ Bonds					
Name of Securities Company					
Account Numbers					
Money Market Funds					
Name of Company					
Types of Accounts/ Account Numbers					
Savings Bonds					
Annuities					
T-Bills					
Cash					

Assets Checklist (Page 3 of 6)

	Amounts	Owned by Husband	Owned by Wife	Owned Jointly	How Titled?
Tax Shelters - Nature and Amounts					
Name of Company					
Account Numbers					
Personal Property - Fair Market Value					
Automobiles					
Boats					
R/V's					
Other Licensed Vehicles					
Antiques					
Jewelry					
Household Furnishings					

Assets Checklist (Page 4 of 6)

		Owned by	Owned by	Owned	How Titled?
	Amounts	Husband	Wife	Jointly	
Business Ownership Interest					
Description and Value					
Notes Receivable					
Employment Benefits					
Name of Companies/ Account Numbers					
Description and Value					
Pension					
IRA					
Profit Sharing					
Stock Options					

Assets Checklist (Page 5 of 6)

	Amounts	Owned by Husband	Owned by Wife	Owned Jointly	How Titled?
Interest in Trust					
Grantor, trustee -value and description					
Powers under trust					
Insurance					
Name of Company/ Policy Numbers					
Health					
Disability					
Homeowners					
Long-term health care					
Licensed Vehicle Insurance Information					
Funeral Insurance					
Potential Inheritance					
From whom, amount, restrictions					

Assets Checklist (Page 6 of 6)

		Owned by	Owned by	Owned	How Titled?
	Amounts	Husband	Wife	Jointly	
Assets for children's education which					
are held in a child's name or otherwise					
Safety Deposit Box					
Name of Bank/ Who are signatories					
Other Assets					
Total Estimated Assets					

Liabilities Checklist (Page 1 of 3)

Liabilities as of					
(Attach copy of statements)					
		Owned by	Owned by	Owned	How Titled?
Liabilities	$ Amount	Husband	Wife	Jointly	
Real Estate - Primary Residence					
Name of Bank/Account Number					
1st Mortgage					
2nd Mortgage					
Real Estate - Secondary Residence					
Name of Bank/Account Number					
1st Mortgage					
2nd Mortgage					
Real Estate - Investment Property					
Name of Bank/Account Number					
1st Mortgage					

Liabilities Checklist (Page 2 of 3)

		Owned by	Owned by	Owned	How Titled?
	$ Amount	Husband	Wife	Jointly	
Vehicle Loans					
Name of Insurance Company Policy Numbers					
Automobiles					
Boats					
R/V's					
Other Vehicles					
Business Loans					
Name of Bank/Account Number					
Personal Loans - Secured					
Name of Bank/Account Number					
Personal Loans - Unsecured					
Name of Bank/Account Number					

Liabilities Checklist (Page 3 of 3)

	$ Amount	Owned by Husband	Owned by Wife	Owned Jointly	How Titled?
Other Liabilities					
Guarantor on Any Loans & Amount					
Total Liabilities					
Total Assets					
Less Total Liabilities					
Net Worth					

NOTE: The following states are considered community property states and distribution of property is handled differently. These states as of September 2012 are: Arizona, California, Idaho, Louisiana, New Mexico, Nevada, Texas, Washington and Wisconsin.

Family Documents (Page 1 of 2)

Family Documents and Advisors			
Name/Addresses/Telephone Number/Contact	Husband	Wife	Jointly
Existing Estate Planning Documents			
Will (date, location of original) who has copies			
Trust (date, location of original) who has copies			
Power of Attorney (date, person to whom powers			
given, nature of power), who has copies			
Medical Power of Attorney (date, person to whom			
powers given), who has copies			
Accountant			
Personal			
Business			
Investment Advisors			
Trust Officers			
Insurance Advisors			
Financial Planners			

Family Documents (Page 2 of 2)

	Husband	Wife	Jointly
Bankers - Personal			
Bankers - Business			
Other Advisors			

www.ingramcontent.com/pod-product-compliance
Lightning Source LLC
Chambersburg PA
CBHW060136050426
42448CB00010B/2148